Also by Charles Reznikoff

Rhythms, 1918
Rhythms II, 1919
Poems, 1920
Uriel Accosta: A Play & A Fourth Group of Verse, 1921
Chatterton, The Black Death, and Meriwether Lewis, 1922 (plays)
Coral and Captive Israel, 1923 (plays)
Nine Plays, 1927
Five Groups of Verse, 1927
By the Waters of Manhattan: An Annual, 1929 (anthology)
By the Waters of Manhattan, 1930 (novel)
Jerusalem the Golden, 1934
Testimony, 1934 (prose)
In Memoriam: 1933, 1934
Early History of a Sewing Machine Operator (with Nathan
    Reznikoff), 1936 (prose)
Separate Way, 1936
Going To and Fro and Walking Up and Down, 1941
The Lionhearted, 1944 (novel)
Inscriptions: 1944-1956, 1959
By the Waters of Manhattan: Selected Verse, 1962
Family Chronicle (with Nathan and Sarah Reznikoff), 1963 (prose)
Testimony: The United States 1885-1890: Recitative, 1965
Testimony: The United States (1891-1900): Recitative, 1968
*By the Well of Living and Seeing and The Fifth Book of the
    Maccabeees,* 1969
*By the Well of Living & Seeing: New & Selected Poems 1918-
    1973,* 1974.

Charles Reznikoff

HOLOCAUST

Black Sparrow Press

Los Angeles • 1975

LIBRARY OF CONGRESS CATALOGING IN PUBLICATION DATA

Reznikoff, Charles, 1894-
  Holocaust.

  Poems.
  1. Holocaust, Jewish (1939-1945)—Poetry. I. Title.
PS3535.E98H6   811'.5'2   75-1269
ISBN 0-87685-232-0
ISBN 0-87685-231-2 pbk.

CONTENTS

HOLOCAUST

All that follows is based on a United States government publication, *Trials of the Criminals before the Nuernberg Military Tribunal* and the records of the Eichmann trial in Jerusalem.

DEPORTATION*

1

One evening, a policeman came and told him—
he had come from Poland and had been in Germany almost thirty
    years—
told him and his family,
"To the police station at once.
But you are going to come back right away," the policeman added.
"Take nothing with you—
except your passports."
When they reached the police station,
they saw Jewish men, women, and children,
some sitting, others standing—
and many in tears.

All were taken to the town's concert hall—
Jews from all areas in town—
and kept there twenty-four hours,
and then taken in police trucks to the railway station.
The streets the trucks went through were crowded
with people shouting,
"The Jews to Palestine! Away to Palestine!"
And the Jews were all put on a train
taking them towards the Polish border.

---

*The National Socialist German Workers Party, known as the Nazis, took over
Germany in January, 1933. Their policy at first was merely to force the Jews to
emigrate.

They came there in the morning—
trains coming from all sorts of places in Germany—
until the Jews numbered thousands.
Here they were searched
and if anybody had more than ten marks
the rest was taken away;
and the S.S.* men, the men of the Nazi protection squads, taking
    it said,
"You didn't bring any more into Germany—
and can't take any more out!"

The men of the S.S. squads were "protecting" them
as they walked towards the Polish border;
whipping those who lingered
and snatching what little baggage anyone had
and shouting "Run! Run!"

When they came to the Polish border, the Polish officials
examined the papers of the Jews,
saw that they were Polish citizens
and took them to a village of about six thousand—
the Jews numbered at least twice as many.

The rain was driving hard
and the Poles had no place to put them
but in stables,
the floors covered with horse dung.

2

A Jew who had come to the office of the city's Jewish
    community
found the office closed
and two men of an S.S. squad with steel helmets and rifles
at the door.
(The two were members of "the entertainment squad"
and did all sorts of things
to amuse themselves and others.)

---

*Schutzstaffel

The Jew was given a bucket of hot water
and told to clean the steps of the entrance;
the water had an acid in it burning his hands.
The chief rabbi of the community, wearing his robe and prayer
    shawl,
was pushed out beside him
and also told to clean the steps;
the other S.S. men, standing around, and passers-by
smiling or laughing.

3

A priest in Germany would find Jews shelter
and Jews came to him to hide.
He sent them to workingmen in the suburbs of Berlin
and to farmers out of town,
and they sheltered hundreds—
not a door was closed.
Telling another priest why he did this,
he asked the priest—who had been in Palestine—
"Do you know the road from Jerusalem to Jericho?"
The priest he spoke to nodded;
and the priest who asked the question went on:
"On this road there was once a Jew
brought down by robbers,
and he who helped him was not a Jew.
The God I worship told me:
'Go and do as he did!' "

INVASION

Five Polish Jews got hold of a small wagon
and hired a Pole to drive them east
to get away from the S.S. men now in the city.
But, when they left the city behind,
suddenly they saw S.S. men
who had been lying in wait for Jews
trying to get away.

The S.S. men ordered the Jews off the wagon
and the five got off.
"Have you any money?" the S.S. men asked
and the five gave whatever they had.
The S.S. men searched them anyway
and then ordered them to take off their clothes
and lie down on the ground
and the S.S. men began to beat them,
changing those who did the beating
and laughing all the time.
Then they ordered the Jews to get on their knees
and sing Hebrew songs;
the Jews sang the Zionist anthem, *Ha-tikvah.*
And then had to crawl through a concrete pipe on the road
before the S.S. men left them.

The five were too.weak after the beatings to go on
and, besides, had no money;
and so went back to the city—
straight to a Jewish hospital.

RESEARCH

We are the civilized—
Aryans;
and do not always kill those condemned to death
merely because they are Jews
as the less civilized might:
we use them to benefit science
like rats or mice:
to find out the limits of human endurance
at the highest altitudes
for the good of the German air force;
force them to stay in tanks of ice water
or naked outdoors for hours and hours
at temperatures below freezing;
yes, study the effects of going without food
and drinking only sea water
for days and days
for the good of the German navy;
or wound them and force wooden shavings or ground glass
into the wounds,
or take out bones, muscles and nerves,
or burn their flesh—
to study the burns caused by bombs—
or put poison in their food
or infect them with malaria, typhus, or other fevers—
all for the good of the German army.
Heil Hitler!

A number of Jews had to drink sea water only
to find out how long they could stand it.
In their torment
they threw themselves on the mops and rags
used by the hospital attendants
and sucked the dirty water out of them
to quench the thirst
driving them mad.

IV

GHETTOS

1

At first there were two ghettos in Warsaw:
one small and the other large,
and between them a bridge.
The Poles had to go under the bridge and Jews over it;
and nearby were German guards to see that the Jews did not mix
    with the Poles.
Because of the German guards,
any Jew who did not take off his hat by way of respect while crossing
    the bridge
was shot—
and many were—
and some were shot for no reason at all.

2

An old man carrying pieces of wood to burn
from a house that had been torn down:
there had been no order against this—
and it was cold.
An S.S. commander saw him
and asked where he had taken the wood,
and the old man answered from a house that had been torn down.
But the commander drew his pistol,
put it against the old man's throat
and shot him.

3

One morning German soldiers and their officers
broke into the houses of the quarter where the Jews had been
   gathered,
shouting that all the men were to come out;
and the Germans took everything in cupboards and closets.
Among the men was an old man in the robe—and wearing the hat—
   of the pious sect of Jews called *Hasidim*.
The Germans gave him a hen to hold
and he was told to dance and sing;
then he had to make believe that he was choking a German soldier
and this was photographed.

4 *

The Jews in the ghetto were swollen with hunger
or terribly thin;
six to eight in a room
and no heating.
Families died during the night
and when neighbors entered in the morning—
perhaps days afterwards—
they saw them frozen to death
or dead from starvation.

Little children were whimpering in the streets
for cold and hunger
to be found in the morning
frozen to death.
Corpses were lying about in the empty streets,
gnawed at by rats;
and crows had come down in flocks
to peck at the bodies.

---

*When the Warsaw ghetto was sealed off by walls, most of the Jews who were left
there had no means of earning their livelihood and families were seen—father,
mother, and children—sitting on the streets. Children would be digging in garbage
cans to find potato peels or anything to chew.

A rumor spread through the ghetto:
the Jews would be taken to another place
with more food, better food, better housing—and work.
Sure enough, this was followed by posters
and orders that those in certain parts of the ghetto
were to bring their luggage, whatever gold and jewels they had,
and food for three days—
but what they brought was not to exceed a certain weight—
and they were to come to a certain square.
Those who disobeyed would be shot.
And the families in the districts named came with their children
　　and luggage.

But a few men jumped off the trains taking them away
and came back to warn the Jews still in the ghetto—
or brought in from elsewhere—
that the trains were not going to a place in which to live
but to die.
And when the same kind of posters were seen again—
for other districts—
people began to hide.
But many went to the square named;
for they really believed they would be resettled:
surely the Germans would not kill healthy people fit to work.

Three o'clock one afternoon
about fifty Jews were in a bunker.
Someone pushed in the sack at the opening
and they heard a voice:
"Come out!
Otherwise we'll throw in a grenade."
The S.S. men and the German police with rods in their hands
were ready
and began beating those who had been in the bunker.
Those who had the strength
lined up as ordered
and were taken to a square

and placed in a single file to be shot.
At the last moment,
a group of other S.S. men came and asked what was going on.
One of those who was ready to shoot answered:
they had pulled the Jews out of a bunker
and were about to shoot them as ordered.
The commander of the second group then said,
"These are fat Jews.
All of them good for soap."
And so they took the Jews to a transport train
which had not yet left for a death camp—
Russian freight cars without steps—
and they had to lift each other into the cars.

7

Among those who had hidden themselves
were four women and a little girl of about seven
hiding in a pit—a dugout covered with leaves;
and two S.S. men went up to the pit and ordered them to
        come out.
"Why did you hide?" they asked
and began to beat the women with whips.
The women begged for their lives:
they were young, they were ready to work.
They were ordered to rise and run
and the S.S. men drew their revolvers and shot all five;
and then kept pushing the bodies with their feet
to see if they were still alive
and to make sure they were dead
shot them again.

8

One of the S.S. men caught a woman with a baby in her arms.
She began asking for mercy: if she were shot
the baby should live.
She was near a fence between the ghetto and where Poles lived
and behind the fence were Poles ready to catch the baby
and she was about to hand it over when caught.

[*28*]

The S.S. man took the baby from her arms
and shot her twice,
and then held the baby in his hands.
The mother, bleeding but still alive, crawled up to his feet.
The S.S. man laughed
and tore the baby apart as one would tear a rag.
Just then a stray dog passed
and the S.S. man stooped to pat it
and took a lump of sugar out of his pocket
and gave it to the dog.

V

MASSACRES*

1

The first day the Germans came into the city
where the young woman lived
they took Jewish men and ordered them to gather the dirt on the
   streets
with their hands.
Then the Jews had to undress
and behind each Jew was a German soldier with a fixed bayonet
who ordered him to run;
if the Jew stopped,
he would be stabbed in the back with the bayonet.
Almost all the Jews came home bleeding—
among them her father.
Later, after the German garrison had left the market place,
large trucks were suddenly there,
and about a dozen soldiers jumped off each truck—
in green uniforms with steel helmets:
these were S.S. men.
They went from house to house
and took Jewish men—young and old—
and brought them to the market place;
here the Jews had to hold their hands on the back of their necks.
About thirty Jews were taken that day;
among them the young woman's father.

---

*By 1941, the policy of the Nazis was changed to extermination of the Jews, not
only in Germany but in all countries the Nazis annexed, invaded or dominated. It
has been estimated that six million Jews lost their lives: about four and a half
million in Poland and in the invaded parts of Russia.

They were then put on one of the trucks and carried off.*
The young woman ran after the truck
until she reached a woods in the neighborhood.
There she found all the Jews who had been taken—
dead.

They had been shot
and were stretched out on the ground
in a pattern:
Jews and Poles
in groups of five
but Jews and Poles in separate groups.
She kissed her father:
he was ice-cold
although it was only an hour after he had been taken.

2

Her father had a shop for selling leather
and was one of the notables in a Polish Jewish community
when the Germans entered.
They put their horses into the synagogue and turned it into a stable.
On a Saturday afternoon, peasants from neighboring villages
came to tell the Jews of the town
that the Germans were killing Jews: they should run away and hide.
But the rabbi and other elders of the town
thought running away useless;
besides, they thought the Germans might take a few of the young
        men to work for them
but that no one would be killed.

The next day, before sunrise, a Jew from a neighboring village
ran into the town shouting:
"Jews, run for your lives!
The Germans are out to kill us,"
and the townspeople saw the Germans coming in.

---

*There was a standing order of the Germans that executions were not to be in a
public place and for this a wooded area was usual.

The young woman's grandfather said, "Run and hide, children,
  but I will stay:
they will do no harm to me."
those who could hid in a neighboring forest.
During the day they heard shooting—
single shots and cries;
but towards evening they thought the Germans would be leaving
  the town
and, sure enough, peasants from the neighborhood met them
and said: "You can go back now.
The Germans killed everybody left behind."

When the Jews came back,
they found that the Germans had rounded up about one hundred and
  fifty Jews,
including the rabbi and other notables.
They told the rabbi to take his prayer shawl along—
the other Jews had been gathered in the center of the town—
and he was told to put on his prayer shawl
and sing and dance. He would not
and was beaten up. And so were the other Jews.
Then they were driven to the cemetery.
Here a shallow grave had been dug for them.
They were told to lie down in fours
and were shot. But her father remained behind in the town—alive:
he had said he was cutting the leather in his shop for shoes
and was registered as a shoemaker.

Later, the Germans went into the town to take whatever they could
  find;
the place was swarming with Germans—four or five to every Jew.
Many were put upon a large truck;
those who could not climb on themselves
were thrown on; and those for whom there was no room on the
  truck
were ordered to run after it.
All the Jews were counted and the Germans searched for every
  missing person on their list.
The young woman was among those who ran,
her little daughter in her arms.
There were those, too, who had two or three children
and held them in their arms as they ran after the truck.
Those who fell were shot—right where they fell.

[35]

When the young woman reached the truck,
all who had been on it were down and undressed and lined up;
the rest of her family among them.
There was a small hill there and at the foot of the hill a dugout.
The Jews were ordered to stand on top of the hill
and four S.S. men shot them—killed each separately.
When she reached the top of the hill and looked down
she saw three or four rows of the dead already on the ground.
Some of the young people tried to run
but were caught at once
and shot right there.
Children were taking leave of their parents;
but her little daughter said to her,
"Mother, why are we waiting? Let us run!"

Her father did not want to take off all of his clothes
and stood in his underwear.
His children begged him to take it off
but he would not and was beaten.
Then the Germans tore off his underwear
and he was shot.
They shot her mother, too,
and her father's mother—
she was eighty years old
and held two children in her arms;
and they shot her father's sister;
she also had babies in her arms
and was shot on the spot.
Her younger sister went up to one of the Germans—
with another girl, one of her sister's friends—
and they asked to be spared,
standing there naked before him.
The German looked into their eyes
and shot them both—her sister and the young friend;
they fell
embracing each other.

The German who had shot her younger sister
turned to her
and asked, "Whom shall I shoot first?"
She was holding her daughter in her arms and did not answer.
She felt him take the child from her;

the child cried out and was shot.
Then he aimed at her: took hold of her hair
and turned her head around.
She remained standing and heard a shot
but kept on standing. He turned her head around again
and shot her;
and she fell into the dugout
among the bodies.

Suddenly she felt that she was choking;
bodies had fallen all over her.
She tried to find air to breathe
and began climbing towards the top of the dugout,
and felt people pulling at her
and biting at her legs.
At last she came to the top.
Bodies were lying everywhere
but not all of them dead:
dying, but not dead;
and children were crying, "Mamma! Papa!"
She tried to stand up but could not.

The Germans were gone.
She was naked,
covered with blood and dirty with the excrement of those in the
    dugout,
and found that she had been shot in the back of the head.
Blood was spurting from the dugout
in many places;
and she heard the cries and screams of those in it still alive.
She began to search among the dead for her little girl
and kept calling her name;
trying to join the dead,
and crying out to her dead mother and father,
"Why didn't they kill me, too?"

She was there all night.
Suddenly she saw Germans on horseback
and sat down in a field
and heard them order all the corpses heaped together;
and the bodies—many who had been shot but were still alive—
were heaped together with shovels.

Children were running about.
The Germans caught the children
and shot them, too;
but did not come near her. And left again
and with them the peasants from around the place—
who had to help—
and the machine-guns and trucks were taken away.

She remained in the field, stretched out.
Shepherds began driving their flocks into the field;
and threw stones at her,
thinking her dead or mad.
Afterwards, a passing farmer saw her,
fed her
and helped her join Jews in the forest nearby.

3

Jewish women were lined up by German troops in charge of the
    territory,
told to undress,
and they stood in their undergarments.
An officer, looking at the row of women,
stopped to look at a young woman—
tall, with long braided hair, and wonderful eyes.
He kept looking at her, then smiled and said,
"Take a step forward."
Dazed—as they all were—she did not move
and he said again: "Take a step forward!
Don't you want to live?"
She took that step
and then he said: "What a pity
to bury such beauty in the earth.
Go!
But don't look backwards.
There is the street to the boulevard.
Follow that."
She hesitated
and then began to walk as told.
The other women looked at her—
some no doubt with envy—

as she walked slowly, step by step.
And the officer took out his revolver
and shot her in the back.

4

The soldier doing the shooting was sitting at the narrow end of
    the pit,
his feet dangling into it;
smoking a cigarette,
the machine-gun on his knees.

As each truck came, those who had been on it—
Jewish men, women, and children of all ages—
had to undress
and put their clothing at fixed places,
sorted in great piles—
shoes, outer clothing, and underwear.

The S.S. man at the pit,
shouted to his comrade
and he counted off twenty, now completely naked,
and told them to go down the steps cut in the clay wall of the pit:
here they were to climb over the heads of the dead
to where the soldier pointed.
As they went towards the pit,
a slender young woman with black hair,
passing a German civilian who was watching,
pointed to herself and said,
"I am twenty-three."
An old woman with white hair
was holding a child about a year old
in her arms,
singing to it and tickling it,
and the child was cooing with delight;
and a father was holding the hand of his little son—
—the child about to burst into tears—
speaking to the child softly,
stroking his head
and pointing to the sky.

Bodies were soon heaped in the large pit,
lying on top of each other,
heads still to be seen and blood running over their shoulders;
but some were still moving,
lifting arms and turning heads.*

5

They gathered some twenty *Hasidic* Jews from their homes,
in the robes these wear,
wearing their prayer shawls, too,
and holding prayer books in their hands.
They were led up a hill.
Here they were told to chant their prayers
and raise their hands for help to God
and, as they did so,
the officers poured kerosene under them
and set it on fire.

---

*There were different techniques: some commanders lined up those to be shot and
had them standing or kneeling on the edge of a pit, facing it; while others had
those to be shot standing with their backs to the pit; and still others had them go
into the pit while still alive and these were shot in the neck while standing or
kneeling. This was the most efficient, for of those shot above the pit all did not fall
into it and then the soldiers had the trouble of pushing them in; but if they were
shot in the pit the next group to be shot could come at once and fall on the bleeding
corpses. But whatever the method of execution it was, to quote an official report,
''always honorable and done in a humane and military manner.''

VI

GAS CHAMBERS AND GAS TRUCKS

1

At night the ghetto was encircled by a large detachment of German
    S.S. squads
and three times as many of the Ukrainian militia;
then the electric lights that had been set up
in and around the ghetto
were switched on.
Four to six men of the squads and the militia
entered each house—or tried to. If the doors and windows were
    closed
and those within did not open at the knocking,
they broke the windows
or forced the doors open with crowbars or beams;
and, if the door of a building was strong
and could not be forced,
the door was blown open by hand grenades.

Those within the houses
were driven into the streets
just as they were
with strokes of whips, kicks, and blows of rifle butts—
it did not matter if they were dressed or in bed—
and forced to run along a road
until they reached a freight train that was waiting.
Car after car was filled
while women and children screamed
and the cracking of whips and rifle shots
sounded and resounded throughout the ghetto
and the cries, "Open the door!"

That no one might get away into the countryside,
this, too, was lit up by rockets.

In the ghetto, corpses of men, women and children
were left in the streets;
the doors of the houses stood open,
windows smashed;
and everywhere
shoes, stockings, jackets and coats, hats and caps.
At the corner of one house lay a baby,
skull crushed
and the wall of the house spattered with its brain and blood.
A farm cart came down a street, drawn by two horses;
dead people with stiff limbs lying on the cart
and legs and arms sticking out over the side boards.

A railroad station with only two platforms
against a hill of yellow sand;
no dead to be seen that day—
or any day if possible;
at any rate, only briefly.
But the smell of the region, even on the main road,
pestilential.
Next to the station, a barracks marked "Cloakroom"
and a door marked "Valuables";
and in the open a corridor, five hundred feet or so long
with barbed wire at both sides
and a signboard, "To the baths."
At the end, a house like a bathhouse
with concrete troughs to the right and left
in which geraniums were growing,
and on the roof the star of David in copper.
After climbing a small staircase,
three small rooms,
hardly six feet in height.

In the morning the freight train arrived—forty-five cars;
almost seven thousand had boarded it
but now some were dead.
When the train stopped, two hundred Ukrainians, doing as they
      were ordered,
opened the doors

and with leather whips
drove the living out.
Then, through a loud speaker, all who had come on the train were
     ordered to undress
and hand over eyeglasses and false teeth—
nothing to be wasted!—
and a little Jewish boy handed out pieces of string to everyone
to tie their shoes in pairs.
All money and whatever valuables they had
were to be handed in at the door marked "Valuables"
and women and girls were to go to the "hairdressers"
who with one or two strokes
cut off their hair
and this was put into large bags and to be used for mats—
nothing lost or wasted!
Then men and women were marched along the corridor between
     the barbed wire:
naked men and women,
mothers with babies at their breast,
frightened children of all ages—
and behind them Ukrainians with guns.

A policeman was telling them in a strong deep voice:
"Nothing whatever will happen to you!
All you have to do is:
breathe deeply!
The inhalation will strengthen your lungs!
A necessary measure against contagious diseases!
And a very good disinfectant!"
If someone stopped to ask what would become of them,
he answered: "The men will have to work, of course,
building streets and houses;
but the women will not have to.
If they wish they can help in the kitchen."
But a woman screamed at the police captain who was watching,
"The blood of my children on your head!"
And he lashed her across the face with his whip
and drove her into the gas chamber.
"Naked in winter," one of the German civilians watching said to
     the Professor of Public Health—
standing beside him—
"enough to kill them."

[45]

"That's what they are here for," the Professor answered drily.

In the gas chambers
the police wedged the people closely together
until men and women were standing on the feet of each other—
and the doors were closed.
But the engine to furnish the gas
could not start.
An hour and two and almost three went by,
and in the gas chambers cries were heard
and many were praying.
The Professor who had been holding his ear against one of the
     wooden doors
turned away, smiled and said, "Just like a synagogue."
And then the engine started working:
in about half an hour
all inside the gas chambers were dead.

When the rear doors were opened,
those inside were standing like statues:
there had been no room to fall
or even bend.
Among the dead, families were to be seen,
holding each other by the hand,
hands tightly clasped
so that those who threw out the dead
had trouble parting them.

The bodies were thrown out quickly
for other transports were coming:
bodies blue, wet with sweat and urine, legs covered with excrement,
and everywhere the bodies of babies and children.
Two dozen workers were busy
opening the mouths of the dead with iron hooks
and with chisels taking out teeth with golden caps;
and elsewhere other workers were tearing open the dead
looking for money or jewels that might have been swallowed.
And all the bodies were then thrown into the large pits dug near the
     gas chambers
to be covered with sand.

At a dinner to honor the officials of this camp—and others like it—
the Professor of Public Health was making a speech:
"Your task is a duty, useful and necessary.
Looking at the bodies of all those Jews
one understands the greatness of your good work—
all its greatness! *Heil Hitler!*"
And the guests shouted, *"Heil Hitler!"*

2

When a transport came and the people were led into the courtyard
    where they had to undress
and go to the gas chambers,
they would sometimes shout and would not move;
and the S.S. man in charge would shout back: "Quiet! Calm down!
I know you want to die,
but first you must work!"
Sometimes the trick was successful;
the people undressed and moved on.

3

The road at Treblinka from Camp One to Camp Two—
where the gas chambers were—
was known as the "Judenstrasse", that is, the "Jews' Street".
At Camp Two S.S. men were posted:
they had dogs, whips, and bayonets.
The Jews on their way to the gas chambers
at first—in the summer of 1942—
walked calmly:
they did not know what they were going to.
But when they entered a gas chamber
stood near the entrance.
There were two Ukrainians near it
who were to turn on the gas that came from a diesel engine;
and the fumes would come out of a pipe
into the chamber.
The last of the Jews to come
did not want to enter at all
sensing evil.

[47]

But the guards pushed them inside,
stabbing with their bayonets,
until the gas chamber was jammed—
so jammed it was difficult to close the door.
When the door was locked
and the gas turned on,
those outside heard screams,
and cries for ''Mamma'' and ''Papa'' from the children,
and prayers in Hebrew.
After about thirty-five minutes,
those inside were dead.
And the officer in charge speaking to those who were to take out
    the bodies
would say, ''Everyone's asleep: take out the bodies!''

They began burning the corpses in 1943.
In January of that year, after a group of senior officers of the Nazis
    had visited the camp,
orders were given to dig up the bodies.
Steam-shovels dumped them on the ground
and with the help of stretchers made of wood
those who worked at getting rid of them
threw the bodies—or parts of bodies—
into the furnaces
or upon grills made of rails
on which the dead were burnt to ashes.

4

Afterwards, gas trucks were also placed at the disposal of the
    commander:
a three-ton truck held about thirty or forty people.
Women and children were lured into these trucks
by the announcement that they also were to be resettled
and there would meet husbands or fathers.
Once inside the truck,
the door was automatically closed
and the driver stepping on the accelerator
sent the gas from the engine
into the truck.
By the time the truck reached the place it was headed for,

[48]

all inside were dead;
and here they did join husbands and fathers,
also dead,
shot by the rifles of the commandos in charge.

5

He was on the shift
meeting the transports that came at night.
Once a transport came from Poland—
those on transports from Czechoslovakia or Hungary had been more
    gullible—
many on this knew what they were coming to.
Some had kept trying to jump out of the trains
and were shot at.
When the first train came in,
those on the night shift saw people hanging out of the windows;
they had been jammed into the cars;
some had simply been suffocated
and there were corpses all around inside.
The night shift had never seen so many crammed together
on any other transport;
and there were more S.S. men than usual about.

Jews on the night shift were standing by
until they heard, "Jews to the cars!"
And then, beaten and shouted at, they went into the cars
to take out the dead.
It was extremely hot and stuffy inside,
and at least four of the shift were working in each car.
As always, S.S. men were walking about with pistols loaded
to shoot at those too weak to climb the steps leading to the vans.
And one of those on the night shift
saw a girl about ten
coming from a heap of dead bodies
and beginning to walk feebly —
an S.S. man shot her in the neck;
saw a little boy,
half naked,
quietly sitting in the middle of the path.
The S.S. man, head of his group—

the Jews among themselves called him "grandfather"
because he was elderly—
tried to shoot the little boy in the neck.
The little boy turned his head
and just managed to say the first two words of the prayer orthodox
    Jews about to die say
when he was killed,
and his body thrown on one of the trucks.

A Jew on the same shift
saw his brother among those who came
and begged the head of the S.S. men
to let his brother go into the camp and live
instead of going straight to the gas chambers.
The S.S. commander listened indifferently
and then said,
"You can go along with him if you like."

VII

WORK CAMPS

1

The state is to get hold of those who never had—
or no longer have—
a right to live in the state,
and the state must turn their strength while it lasts
to the good of the state.
They must be fed, sheltered, and treated in such a way
as to use them as much as possible
at the lowest possible cost.

Get as much work as possible from the young and strong
in concentration camps—
or in factory or field—
and give as little as possible
in clothing or food.
Let those die who cannot keep working fast
or, if they will not work,
hanged
and left swinging
for the others to see.
Heil Hitler!

2

He was then twenty years old and was taken with his mother
from the factory where both worked
to a square in the city
and stood there with many others for hours.
Before night fell

all were put on cars for freight—
crowded, crammed into them.
There was almost no light
and only a small window in the car
and they were choking for air.
The train began to move about eight in the evening.
At dawn it stopped at a station;
the young man and his mother were near the window
and saw Polish railroad workers beckoning to those on the train
and making all kinds of gestures to tell them they were taken to be
    killed.
But the young man did not believe it.
The train moved on again
and when it stopped this time
those on the train heard shouts, "Everybody out!"—
and screams:
the Germans had begun to beat them
and those who did not get off at once were shot.
Many of them—the old and sick and those who had fainted—
were killed in the train or on the platform.
The rest were gathered on the platform with their belongings
and taken to a gate leading to a fenced courtyard.
They were in Treblinka.

When they were gathered again in the courtyard
women were sent to the left, men to the right.
The young man did not want to leave his mother
but he was hit on the head—
it may have been by a stick—
and fell to the ground.
When he got up his mother was gone
and he never saw her again.
Out of that transport, about four hundred young men were selected.

At the end of the camp where the gas chambers were
was a big dugout;
it was fenced off by barbed wire
and near the entrance was a hut painted white
with a Red Cross and the inscription "Lazarette"—
German for a kind of hospital—
on the wall.
Some of the young men who were left of the transport

had to throw corpses into this dugout—
those killed on the railroad platform,
as well as those who had fainted but were still alive.
The young man who had come with his mother
had to help sort out the belongings of those taken to the gas
    chambers:
clothing, shoes, tools, medicines, and children's toys—
everything piled high in the courtyard.
And the transports were arriving all the time;
large transports daily—even twice a day.
Flower beds were later set up around the platform to which the
    transports came;
and there were signs with arrows reading "To the train" or "To
    Bialystock,"
a city known for the number of Jews who lived—or rather had
    lived—there;
so that those arriving would not know at first where they were:
it looked like a kind of transit station, a railway junction.

Some of the young men working in the camp tried to escape
but most were caught;
hanged by their feet
and S.S. men and Ukrainians would come and whip them;
and finally an S.S. man shot them dead.

3

When the Second World War began
he was living in Lodz with his mother.
The family was hungry
and his mother became bloated from hunger—
as many were.
His mother and her family escaped from the ghetto in Lodz
and fled to the Warsaw ghetto;
but there it became much worse:
his mother had sold everything she had
and they had nothing to eat.
She then told him to get to the Lublin area
where other members of the family lived,
and he escaped to a small town.

One morning he heard cries and shrieking:
the Germans were taking the Jews to the market place.
They crowded them into freight cars
and he was among them.
There was hardly room to stand
and many fainted.
But the journey took only two or three hours
and they were brought to a death camp.
When they got off the train
they were hurried to a small gate,
the S.S. men shouting, "Hurry! Hurry!"
and there the men were taken from the women and children.
While this was going on
a band was playing.

The men stayed there all night
but the women and children were taken at once to the gas chambers.
Many of the Jews had not believed there would be any mass
    extermination—
a few murders, of course;
and even when they were jammed into the freight cars,
many were happy not to be going to a camp they knew to be a hard
    labor camp
and going eastward instead:
it had been rumored that they would be taken to the Ukraine to work
    in the fields
now that Germany had taken over most of it.
But some remembered a Jew who had come to town and said:
"Do not believe what you are told.
The Jews are not being taken to the Ukraine;
they are sent to death camps—
and killed there."
But nobody believed him;
they thought he was just trying to start a panic.
And even in the camp they had now been sent to—
a few hundred feet from the gas chambers—
the men were told by the Germans that in a few weeks they would
    rejoin their families.
They saw the belongings of the women and children piled up;
but the Germans said:
"They are getting new clothes.
You are going to be gathered together and then sent to the
    Ukraine."

There were really three camps at that camp:
one for shoemakers, tailors, and other craftsmen;
another for those who worked at sorting the clothes of those who
    came in the transports and were gassed;
and the third camp where the gas chambers were.
The morning after the arrival of the Jewish men who had just come,
the Germans began to sort them:
choosing the young and able-bodied by saying, ''du''—the German
    familiar for ''you''.
In about half an hour most of the men who had come in that
    transport
had been taken to the gas chambers
and only about a hundred and fifty were left to work;
the young man who had fled from Warsaw to the Lublin area
    among them.

He was put to work taking and piling up the clothing of the people
    who had come—
and were coming—in the transports
and kept seeing that many who had come disappeared.
After the young man had worked for a while the first day,
he was dazed
and as he stood, dazed and benumbed—
he was only fifteen then—
a Jew came up to him and said, ''My boy, if you are going to
    behave this way, you are not going to survive here.''

When they had come from work that day,
the officer in charge put them through a roll call
and told them that the people who had disappeared had been sent
    to the Ukraine.
Then he said, ''Who is sick? Who is tired? Who doesn't want
    to work?
Let him step out of line.''
A number did. They knew what was going to happen to them
but were fed up with what had happened
and one of them said to those who stayed in line,
''Oh, don't work! You can have a good rest.''
The same routine was carried out every evening.
In a month, of the hundred and fifty in the group the lad was in to
    begin with
only about fifty were left.

[57]

Once a transport came from another camp.
Something had gone wrong with the gas chambers there
and those who came spent the night in the open courtyard.
They were almost skeletons:
did not care about anything
and could hardly speak.
When beaten, they just sighed.
The Jews working in the camp
were ordered to give them food;
but those who had come had trouble just sitting up
and stepped on each other
to get what little food they were given.
Next morning they were taken to the gas chambers.

In the courtyard where they had spent the night
were several hundred dead.
Jews of the camp they had come to were told:
"Undress the bodies
and carry them to the wagons."
But these Jews were too weak to carry the bodies on their shoulders
and had to drag them,
take them by the feet and drag them along;
and the Germans beat those who dragged
to go faster.
One Jew left the body he was dragging to rest for a moment
and the man he thought dead
sat up,
sighed and said in a weak voice,
"Is it far?"
The Jew dragging him
stooped and put his hand gently around the man's shoulder
and just then felt a whip on his back:
an S.S. man was beating him.
He let go of the body—
and went on dragging the man to the wagons.

4

There were articles in the Slovakian press
about what was happening to the Jews deported from Poland and
    Slovakia:
they were well and safe

and there were pictures of gay faces and smiling girls.
One day Jewish women in Slovakia
were gathered in a cellar
and, finally, taken in freight cars to Auschwitz.

In the part of the camp in which they were placed,
there were two women on each narrow bed.
And they were all sent out to work: to dig beets from the ground
where the beets had been rotting for years,
left there by the Poles.
Sometimes they came upon a good plot;
but if anyone dared to take one of those beets to her mouth,
it meant death at once.
And sometimes they did work they did not understand why they
    were told to do it:
straightening out a hill in a field
or taking a mound of earth from one place to another.
Work for them began when the stars were still in the sky;
and when the day's work ended it was dark.

A woman came with her little daughter
and S.S. men were there one morning
and took the child away:
a mother was forbidden to keep her child with her.
Later, the woman found out that her child had been thrown into
    the fire
in which the dead were being burnt,
and that night threw herself against the electrified barbed wire fence
    around the camp.

In another camp to which Jewish women had been taken
they were set to work carrying building materials,
wooden beams and the like.
There was a quarry below
and the women had also to bring rocks to where new roads were
    being paved—
only women worked at that:
they were harnessed to the long ropes attached to wagons
and had to drag them up a steep incline—
whatever the weather—
twelve hours a day,
wearing wooden shoes that would slip in the mud and snow.

5

Trucks from Belgium reached the concentration camp at last:
when the doors were opened,
a stench, almost unbearable;
and the bodies of those within tumbled out—
some dead, the rest unconscious;
the bodies of the dead bloated, reddened and bluish,
eyes protruding from sockets,
clothes soaked with sweat and excrement.

6

Jews from Holland, France, and Hungary, and later from Greece,
were brought to a camp in freight trains or cattle cars—
three or four trains a day—
the cars crowded
and on the road days and nights,
with nothing for those inside
to eat or drink;
and when the cars were at the camp
they were driven out with whips
and blows from the butts of rifles.
They were then lined up before the camp physician
and as they passed before him
he would ask their age of the men—if they did not show it—
and what they did for a living,
and then point with his thumb
to the right or left;
and those sent to the left—all able to work—
were driven barefoot to the camp,
even when snow was on the ground,
and whipped to go faster.
One of the soldiers on guard said as a joke,
pointing to the smoke from the chimneys of the crematorium,
"The only road from here to freedom!"

Some of those sent to the right
would be loaded on vans
with only a single mmber of an S.S. squad
seated in front
and were gassed in the van—

if it was that kind—
and their bodies brought straight to the crematorium.
But most would be brought to the gas chambers
behind trees that had been cut down
and set up in rows.

If the gas chambers were crowded
and no room for the youngest children—or even adults—
they were thrown on piles of wood
that had been sprinkled with gasoline
and just burnt alive.
But that their screams might not be too disturbing
to those who worked
an orchestra of Jews from the camp
was set to playing loudly
well-known German songs.

7

When the train on which an old doctor who had been a colonel in
    the Austrian army
came to the death camp,
he showed his diplomas
and pictures of himself as colonel;
but this did not save him.
The S.S. men beat him until he died
and tore up his diplomas.

8

The day's routine began, in the summer, at four in the morning;
in the winter at six.
They were marched to the parade ground of the camp,
where the roll-call by numbers and not by names
was held, and a report made of those who had died in the night.
Then in columns of five they were marched to where they were
    working—
a stone quarry, a clay pit, an ammunition factory, or a construction
    job.
When the day's work was done,

each in one camp—or several—had to pick up stones or bricks,
at least ten pounds in weight,
to carry back to the camp.
Perhaps merely to show they were strong enough
to work the next day.
Back at camp
they were assembled again for another roll-call
and then the punishments were carried out:
floggings between five and twenty-five lashes
and sometimes on every tenth man.

In one camp after they were awakened at four in the morning
and got a cup of coffee
they worked in the quarries all day
and returned to the camp at nine or ten at night.
They then got a bowl of watery soup
and two or three bad potatoes.
By the time they got to the bundles of straw on which they slept
it was midnight.
In two months, thirty-five hundred in that camp died of hunger.

9

Among the S.S. men there were exceptions.
Some of the Jews in that camp
were working at laying a narrow-gauge railroad
to be used for carting bodies;
and the man in charge would kill with his hammer.
But one day there was another man in charge.
Much as those working were afraid of the S.S.,
a new man might be worse;
and when they saw a new man, a senior officer at that,
they were, to say the least, uneasy.
One of the Jews had loaded sections of rail on his back
and the new S.S. man said: "Why do you take so many?"
So the Jew took off one
but the S.S. man had him take off a few and said;
"There's time. Walk slowly."
The Jews saw him when the transports came—
walking about and looking ashamed.
Sometimes he would say a kind word to them.

But he only stayed a month;
one evening he came into their barracks and said:
"I didn't know where I was being sent to.
I didn't know about this,
and when I found out I asked at once for a transfer.
I am leaving you now,"
and he shook hands with some of the Jews
and wished them to survive.

10

Many a woman in Germany, whose husband had been sent to a
    concentration camp
and killed there,
would get the following message which her husband had been
    ordered to write:
"Feeling well and like it here."
Or "Your husband has died of a heart attack;
we are sending you an urn with his ashes
and for this send us three marks and a half."

VIII

CHILDREN

1

Once, among the transports, was one with children—two freight
    cars full.
The young men sorting out the belongings of those taken to the
    gas chambers
had to undress the children—they were orphans—
and then take them to the "lazarette."
There the S.S. men shot them.

2

A large eight-wheeled car arrived at the hospital
where there were children;
in the two trailers—open trucks—were sick women and men
lying on the floor.
The Germans threw the children into the trucks
from the second floor and the balconies—
children from one-year-old to ten;
threw them upon the sick in the trucks.
Some of the children tried to hold on to the walls,
scratched at the walls with their nails;
but the shouting Germans
beat and pushed the children towards the windows.

The children arrived at the camp in buses,
guarded by gendarmes of the French Vichy government.
The buses stopped in the middle of the courtyard
and the children were quickly taken off
to make room for the buses following.
Frightened but quiet,
the children came down in groups of fifty or sixty to eighty;
the younger children holding on to older ones.
They were taken upstairs to empty halls—
without any furniture
and only dirty straw bags on the floor, full of bugs:
children as young as two, three, or four years of age,
all in torn clothes and dirty,
for they had already spent two or three weeks in other camps,
uncared for;
and were now on their way to a death camp in Poland.
Some had only one shoe.
Many had diarrhea
but they were not allowed in the courtyard
where the water-closets were;
and, although there were chamber pots in the corridor of each story,
these were too large for the small children.

The women in the camp who were also deportees
and about to be taken to other camps
were in tears:
they would get up before sunrise
and go into the halls where the children were—
in each a hundred to a hundred and twenty—
to mend the children's clothing;
but the women had no soap to clean the children,
no clean underwear to give them,
and only cold water with which to wash them.
When soup came for the children,
there were no spoons;
and it would be served in tins
but the tins were sometimes too hot for the children to hold.

After nine at night no one—except for three or four who had a
    permit—

was allowed to stay with the children.
Each room was then in darkness,
except for one bulb painted blue by blackout instructions.
The children would wake at night
calling for their mothers
and would then wake each other,
and sometimes all in the room would start crying out
and even wake the children in other rooms.

A visitor once stopped one of the children:
a boy of seven or eight, handsome, alert and gay.
He had only one shoe and the other foot was bare,
and his coat of good quality had no buttons.
The visitor asked him for his name
and then what his parents were doing;
and he said, "Father is working in the office
and Mother is playing the piano."
Then he asked the visitor if he would be joining his parents soon—
they always told the children they would be leaving soon to rejoin
      their parents—
and the visitor answered, "Certainly. In a day or two."
At that the child took out of his pocket
half an army biscuit he had been given in camp
and said, "I am keeping this half for Mother;"
and then the child who had been so gay
burst into tears.

4

Other children, also separated from their parents,
arrived in buses,
and were put down in the courtyard of the camp—
a courtyard surrounded by barbed wire
and guarded by gendarmes.
On the day of leaving for the death camp
they were awakened at five in the morning.
Irritable, half asleep, most of them refused to get up and go down to
      the courtyard.
Women—French volunteers, for they were still in France—
urged the children gently
to obey—they must!—and vacate the halls.

[69]

But many still would not leave the straw bags on which they slept
and then the gendarmes entered,
and took up the children in their arms;
the children screamed with fear,
struggled and tried to grasp each other.

5

Women guards at the women's section of the concentration camp
were putting little children into trucks
to be taken away to the gas chambers
and the children were screaming and crying, ''Mamma, Mamma,''
even though the guards were trying to give them pieces of candy to
    quiet them.

ENTERTAINMENT

1

The commander of a camp, among his amusements, as in other
    camps
had a large dog
and at the cry of "Jude," that is, "Jew,"
the dog would attack the man and tear off pieces of flesh.
In another camp, the Jews who had just come
kept seeing a dog—
the dog belonged to the S.S. man in charge of "the showers,"
    that is, the gas chambers;
the S.S. man would call the dog "Mensch," that is, "man":
and whenever he set the dog on a Jew would say, "Man, get that
    dog!"

2

In one camp the officers, for their amusement,
if they saw a group of Jews at a distance,
would draw their revolvers and shoot in that direction;
but they must have shot into the air
because no one was ever hit.
Throwing stones at the group was another matter:
some would be hurt—in the face, hands or legs.
But, in another camp, the two commanders began a game:
they would stand at their windows
and, while those carrying stones were passing,
the two would shoot at them, aiming at the tip of a nose or a finger;
and in the evening would pick out those who had been hit
and were no longer any good for work

and have them shot.
And in still another camp the officers played "the spinning top":
they would place a stick in the ground—stand it up quite low—
and the man to be tortured would have to keep touching it with his
    right hand,
his left hand behind his back,
and keep turning around the stick,
and as he ran around he was beaten
and those beating him would shout, "Quicker! Quicker!"
He would have to go around at least ten times,
but after three or four times some would faint.

3

Once the commander of a camp had eight of the strongest among
    the Jews
placed in a large barrel of water,
saying that they did not look clean,
and they had to stand in this barrel naked for twenty-four hours.
In the morning, other Jews had to cut away the ice:
the men were frozen to death.
In this camp—and in others also—
they had an orchestra of Jews
who had to play every morning and evening
and whenever Jews were taken to be shot.
In one such camp,
the orchestra had all of sixty men.

4

Once a group of Jews who came on a truck
were ordered off when they reached a camp at night
and a powerful light was suddenly focused upon them.
They were told to keep looking towards it.
When they tried to look aside
an S.S. man stabbed them to death.

The Germans in another camp, too, had their games.
A young man would be sent to close an umbrella open on a roof
and had to climb to do it;

if he fell he was beaten to death.
One after another had to climb to the roof
to close the umbrella
and almost all fell down,
and each who fell was beaten to death;
and a dog would bite the man at each stroke.
Then there were times when the inmates had to run
and were shot at.
And once five had the bottoms of their trousers bound with rope
and mice put into the trousers;
the men had to stand at attention
and those who could not because of the mice
were beaten.

On Sundays there was no work and Jews would be placed in a row:
each had a bottle on his head
and the S.S. men amused themselves by shooting at the bottles.
If a bottle was hit,
the man lived;
but if the bullet landed below,
well, the man had it.

MASS GRAVES

1

About thirty Jews were taken to Chelmno
by the S.S.,
looking for strong, husky men.
At night the S.S. went around town
and grabbed people out of their beds
and took them to the headquarters of the German police.
They were then put on a truck
and S.S. men with machine guns followed them to Chelmno.
There they were put into a cellar.
On the first night, one of those in the cellar lit a little candle
and read the inscriptions on a wall:
"No one leaves this place alive"
and "When people are taken to work,
they are taken to be shot."

Next morning, when they were still in the cellar,
they heard a truckload of people arriving in the courtyard
and a voice saying:
"Now you are going to the bathhouse;
you will get new clothes and go out to work;"
and some of those in the truck began clapping their hands:
glad that they were to work—and live.
But soon those in the cellar could hear screams from the truck
as the engine began working and the gas flowed in;
and then the screams died down.

Five of the Jews were taken from the cellar
to put in a room—full of clothing and shoes—

the clothing and shoes left behind.
And the rest in the cellar
were sent to the woods
and set to digging trenches.
They would leave early in the morning
when it was still dark, for it was winter;
and when the trucks arrived
they had to wait until the fumes of the gas were gone
and then five or six would open the doors,
take out the dead
and put them right in the trenches.
One of the Jews working there
recognized a man of his own town
and remembered him as healthy and strong.
He still showed signs of life
and one of the guards shot him in the head.
Then the Ukrainians working for the Germans would come—
a Ukrainian and a German, always in pairs—
and the Ukrainians had pliers in their hands
and pulled out the gold teeth of the dead
and took off the gold rings;
and if a ring did not come off easily,
would cut off the finger.
And then there were Jews whose work it was
to place the bodies so that they formed a single layer:
a head on one side and the feet of the next body on the same side.

After the Jew who had recognized the man from his home town
had been working in the woods for some time,
other Jews from his own town were among the dead
and among them—
his wife and his two children!
He lay down next to his wife and children and wanted the Germans
    to shoot him;
but one of the S.S. men said:
"You still have enough strength to work,"
and pushed him away.
That evening he tried to hang himself
but his friends in the cellar would not let him
and said, "As long as your eyes are open,
there is hope."
The next day the man who had tried to die was on a truck.

They were still in the woods
and he asked one of the S.S. men for a cigarette.
He himself did not smoke usually
but he lit the cigarette and, when he was back where his companions
    were sitting, said:
"Look here! He gives out cigarettes.
Why don't you all ask him for a cigarette?"
They all got up—
they were in the back of the truck—
and went forwards
and he was left behind.
He had a little knife
and made a slit in the tarpaulin at the side
and jumped out;
came down on his knees
but got up and ran.
By the time the S.S. men began shooting
he was gone in the woods.

2

He was taken out of the camp he was in
for "road building."
But it was not for road building:
it was to hide traces of the Nazi murders during the past three years.
As at other camps, those at work would uncover a mass grave;
take out the bodies
and pile them up in tiers
and burn them;
look for whatever valuables could be found in the ashes,
such as gold teeth and rings,
and grind the bones;
and then throw the ashes into the air
and put back the earth that had been dug up
and plant seeds on it.
Sometimes when they picked up a body—
among those who had just been shot—
and put it on the fire,
the body began to scream
because the person was still alive.
That is why among the bodies dug up

some had their mouths open and tongues out:
they had been buried alive
and had choked to death.

Those digging up the dead
had to be careful:
no hair or piece of bone to be left
or even a piece of paper—
everything to be burnt
so that nobody would know there had ever been a grave there.
The heap of the dead sometimes had as many as two thousand
        bodies,
but an exact count was kept of the number of bodies burnt;
in the evening those working at it had to report the number to the
        commander in charge—
and were forbidden to tell it to anyone else.
If one of them was asked, even by the man who kept the account,
"How many bodies were burnt yesterday?"
he always answered, "I forget."
Otherwise, his body would be added to the dead.

3

In the morning the Jews were lined up by an officer
and the officer told them:
"You are Jews, unworthy of life,
but are now supposed to work."
They were put upon trucks
and taken away to a forest
and set to digging.
After two or three spadefuls of earth,
the spade of one hit something hard,
and he saw that it was the head of a human being.
There was also a bad smell all around.
He stopped digging
and the officer in charge came towards him shouting:
"Why did you stop?
Didn't you know there are bodies buried here?"
He had opened a mass grave.

[*82*]

There were about ten thousand dead in that grave.
And after they had dug up the bodies
they were told to burn them.
Planks had been brought and beams—long and heavy.
The Germans also brought a grinding machine to grind the bones
and the ground bones would be sieved
for the gold fillings of teeth.
The dust of the bones would then be spread over the fields,
and the smell was dreadful.

They kept on working three months
opening mass graves;
and opened eight or nine.
In one those digging saw a boy of two or three,
lying on his mother's body.
He had little white shoes on
and a little white jacket,
and his face was pressed against his mother's.

One grave would remain open for new corpses
coming all the time;
a truck would bring the bodies, still warm,
to be thrown into the grave—
naked as Adam and Eve;
Jewish men, many of them bearded, and Jewish women and
    children.
The graves they had opened would be refilled with earth
and they had to plant grass all over them;
as for the dead—
a thousand bodies would be put on a pyre;
and there were two pyres of bodies burning all the time.

XI

MARCHES

1

With the Russians advancing on the camp,
there were no trains to transport those who worked there
and they were marched westward.
They could not go the usual way to the camp they were headed for
because this was for the German army,
and had to go across fields deep in snow which reached to their hips.
The S.S. men with them were in a bad mood
because they, too, were not used to conditions such as these
and would sometimes shoot one of the Jews as a whim.
Whoever was shot would be covered with snow at once,
because the snow was falling.

2

After an attack by the Russians
the Jews had to leave and march to another camp;
walk in the snow in their wooden shoes,
sometimes sinking in snow or mud up to their knees.
In a short time many could not walk;
and the S.S. men who followed in a car
shot all who fell or lagged behind;
sometimes even shot at those who walked to make them run.
Many went barefoot
because they could not wear the wooden shoes.
In their thirst they picked up snow and lapped at it.
At the entrance of the camp to which they finally came—
those who lived through the march—
there was a great heap of bodies at the entrance:
those in charge of the camp had not bothered to bury them.

In the camp they were lined up for a roll-call;
stood there all night, stark naked in the cold,
waiting for the S.S. men to come.
After the roll-call in the morning,
under blows, right and left, from rifle butts and clubs,
the S.S. men shouting, "Hurry! Hurry!",
they were driven to pits where other inmates were lying
simply on the ground, without blankets,
and were told to stay there until further orders.

Their work, it turned out, was to bring bags of cement—
run with them.
It was cold: no underwear,
only a thin shirt,
and some took one of the bags to wear;
and all had only the wooden shoes that rubbed their feet.
Everybody was saying, "Whoever is placed here
will die here."
At times a German guard would come over to a man who could not
        lift the weight he had to
and say to him kindly: "Take it easy. Rest a while."
And when the Jew would sit down,
would shoot him.

They were again placed in long rows
but only three abreast,
and started marching again
and saw along the road
blood—but no corpses.
But they were told that they must not look
left or right or backwards—
only forwards.

Three bearded Jews among them
were suddenly taken out.
When the third man was taken,
his son cried, "Leave my father alone:
I will take his place.
Take me!"
The S.S. man taking his father said,
"You come, too!"
And all four were shot in the back of the head:
the bullets coming out of their foreheads.

[88]

The shooting went on.
The S.S. men would take a man out of line,
hit him with the butts of their rifles
and shoot him.
Those who were shooting kept changing—
they were changed every half hour—
and the Jews in line were kept running,
the S.S. men shouting in Polish,
"Quicker! Quicker!"
When they reached the next village
those who did the shooting
would ask each other,
"How many did you get?"
Some answered, "Eighty-nine;" and others, "A hundred," "A
    hundred and two."

When they reached the village where they were to spend the night,
the Jews were put into a large hall;
but the hall was not large enough for all of them,
and they were packed so closely they could hardly move
and, at that, others were in the corridors.
One of them had some bread
and divided it among five of those nearest him
and, though each had only a small piece,
they could not swallow it,
for their throats were dry with thirst
and they were tired, dead tired.

On the third day they were again set marching,
three abreast,
and every other minute heard shooting.
The S.S. men would put their hands on a man
and tell him to lie down to shoot him
and if he would not
he would be hit on the head with a rifle butt;
but most were so tired
they could not resist.
Finally, they reached a suburb of the city they were headed for
and here the Jews were told to sit down and start singing Jewish
    songs.
Whoever would not sit down and sing, they were told, would be
    shot;
so they sat down and began singing.

ESCAPES

1

Later, in October of 1944, the S.S. men began to empty the camp
    at Chelmno
but a hundred Jews were ordered to stay behind to work.
The gas trucks went towards Kelle,
and those who were left behind
began to take everything apart.

On a night in January,
those working there
heard a truck at the gate.
It was opened and two S.S. men came in.
One had a flashlight and shouted at the Jews,
"Five men follow me!"
They were taken out and those left behind heard five shots.
Then the other S.S. man came in and shouted,
"Five more—out!"
After the fourth group of five had been taken out and shot,
the S.S. man came in again.
But one of those left behind
was hiding behind the door,
a knife in his hand.
He jumped on the S.S. man and stabbed him,
broke his flashlight,
and stabbed him again and again.
He was shot in the foot
but ran into the neighboring woods and escaped.

There were over a hundred Jews in the car of the train he was in—
not enough room even to stand without crowding;
and in the evening the train left.
When morning came they saw that the train was going east:
a few small railway stations, forests, hills and mountains;
but they did not know just where they were.
He wanted to stick his head out of the window and see the signposts
    at the stations
but they had been told they must not look out
and he was afraid the guard on top of the train
would shoot.
In the car women were fainting
and in one corner were cries of ''Water, water!''
But there was none,
and they had no food for two days.

After three days and nights the train pulled into a side track—
they still did not know where they were—
and they were kept in the train for hours.
When they were let off they saw the smoke of furnaces
and there was a stench in the air.
Some asked those who were on the platform what the strange smell
    was
and they said it came from burning rags.
But when a Jew who had been on the train said,
''I have forgotten my prayer shawl and phylacteries in the car,''
someone said, ''What do you need them for?
In a little while you will be going over there,''
and pointed to the furnaces.
They were in Auschwitz.

He had been in the train with his parents
and his brothers and a sister:
four brothers, one fifteen, another eleven, his sister eight years old,
another brother six,
and a baby brother.
A German officer at the station was pointing to the right or to
    the left;
his parents were sent to the right—
he did not even have time to take leave of them—

and he to the left.
His brothers and sister went with his parents
and he never saw any of them again.

In January, 1945, he was on the day shift of a coal mine in Silesia
and coming back from the mine in the evening
suddenly an order came to line up and leave the camp.
Where to?
They did not know.
They had no time to wash or eat.
And those working in the camp—about three thousand Jews—
began to march.
They walked for twenty-four hours;
it was cold, snowing, and they had not eaten.
Some fainted and were shot,
their bodies left by the wayside.

In the evening of the next day
they came to a town where there was another labor camp
and were told to sit by the road in the snow
and wait.
They waited about two hours
and then the commandant of the camp—or a deputy—
came and told them:
"Those who cannot carry on will stay behind:
trucks will come and pick them up."
About two hundred stayed—
he among them—
in the snow and cold and without food.

In the morning the Jews who had stayed
were led into a kind of dining-hall
and again told to wait.
Then they were taken out of town,
given spades and told to dig.
S.S. men and others were standing behind them
with whips in their hands,
whipping them all the time.
They kept digging with what strength they had left
all day
and were then taken back to the dining-hall.
The following morning a lieutenant of the S.S. came and said,

"I know you are very hungry;"
for three days they had been given no food.
"When the miners come from the night shift,
you will get whatever food is left."
When he ended,
a large pot was brought into the room.

By this time other Germans were present,
some in green uniforms and many in black.
The lieutenant took those Jews who had stayed behind,
one after the other,
put the head of each into the pot—
and fired a bullet into the nape of the man's neck.
He kept on doing this
until another officer came into the room
and whispered something to him. Then he stopped.
There were only eleven left
of the two hundred. The bodies of those who were killed
were taken by others in the labor camp
to the holes dug the day before.

But the eleven, the young man among them, were taken to a cellar
and there were frozen potatoes
and they ate them.
They spent all night in the cellar
and then they and the other Jews in the camp
were put into open freight cars.
The train moved along for half a day
and stopped near a forest.
They were all brought to the forest and the Germans started
    shooting at them.
He ran—
escaped—
and stayed in the forest two days.
Then the Russians came.

3

One Saturday, when he was thirteen,
he was taking a walk with his father in the ghetto of Lodz;
they heard shots

and saw people falling.
And then his father fell down, too:
shot and killed.
He himself was caught and put on a truck
but begged the men who held him prisoner to let him go home
to tell his mother what had happened
and that he was to go away with them;
but all they answered was, "Shut up!"
(Afterwards, when he was taking out the gold teeth of the dead
    at Chelmno
and had to go through all sorts of files,
he saw a photograph of his mother in one of them.)

When those held on the trucks with him got off in Chelmno,
they were told to put their feet on chairs
and both feet were chained to each other.
The length of the chain was about fifteen inches
and they had trouble walking. They just hopped,
and the chains were left on their feet at night too.

The group he was in first
was told to clean a building that had been bombed
before they came,
and they found bones and skulls and arms and legs scattered about;
and learned, afterwards, that Jews who were sick had been gathered
    in the building
and then it had been blown up.
On the second day of their arrival,
an officer of the S.S. came and told them,
"If you cannot work, tell me so;
and those who can't work will go out into the fresh air."
Nobody spoke up,
but he was back in a few days
and asked again, "Who can't work?"
And one among them said, "It's a little hard for me.
I should like to rest a while.
I would appreciate it."
And the S.S. officer answered,
"I can't send just one man out.
I must send a number out to rest a while."
So a number stepped out of line
and he said, "All right, come with me."

[97]

They followed him
and he told them to lie down—
and shot them dead.

About two or three months after the lad's arrival,
transports of Jews
began to arrive—a great number.
When the first crematorium was ready,
people were loaded into the gas trucks—
about a hundred each—
they had each been given a cake of soap and a towel
and told they were going to take a shower;
then the door of the truck would be tightly closed
and when the truck moved the gas would pour into it—
and they were killed.
The gold teeth and gold fillings would be taken out of their mouths
and the gold rings taken away:
the lad worked at that nearly all the time,
helping a subordinate officer whose name was Walter.

Every fortnight there was a selection from the group the lad was in.
They were asked how long they had been there
and if anyone answered he had been there eight days,
he was sent into the woods
and shot.
The lad himself was there three months,
but whenever he was asked how long he had been there
would answer, ''Two days.''
But finally the S.S. officer questioning him
began to swear at him in German
and said he was lying.
At that he began to cry,
and Walter came up to the officer and said something or other—
the lad didn't know just what—
and after that the officer left him alone.

Together with other Jewish workers
the lad was made to go through an exercise:
an officer would come on Saturdays
and would take four at a time out of a group of fifty
and say, ''You see this finger?
If I move it this way, stand;

and if it moves that way,
lie down.'' It was up and down and up and down
until they were completely out of breath.
Finally, the officer took out his pistol
and shot those who did not stand up and were still lying down.

A Jew who had just come to the camp the day before
was set to work bringing corpses to the crematorium
and saw his sister's corpse among them.
In the evening he went to the garbage dump—
there was not a strong guard there—
and fled.
He managed to take the chain from one of his feet
and reached the river;
but the non-Jew on the ferry
saw the chain on his other foot
and ran back to where there was a German guard
and said, ''There's a Jew escaping!''
The guard went to the bank of the river, found and killed him.

That evening, the commander of the group he had been in told
    them,
''Everybody out!''
The man who had tried to escape was, of course, missing.
Then the commander said, ''Four men out!''
and sent them to the place to which the body had been brought.
They brought the body back
and the commander said, ''You see, he tried to escape.''
Then Walter took the lad who was in the same group as the man
    who had tried to escape
and sent the lad to the camp of the S.S. guards
to scrub the floor. The officer above the commander in charge of
    the group
came and said, ''Fifteen out!''
and took his pistol and killed them.
Then he said, ''Do you know why I did it?
Because a man had run away.
And if any of you tries to run away,
I will kill you all.''
When the lad came back, he was told they had been looking for him
to be one of the fifteen.

They began to disband the camp three months before the Russians
    came.
There were only about eighty Jews left.
One of the German officers said that forty were to be taken to
    another camp:
they would be much better off than in Chelmno.
The forty were put on a truck—
and it went towards the woods.
When the truck came back, the lad was sent by one of the Jews in
    the camp
to look for a note in the truck:
the men who had been sent away had said that if they were sent to
    the woods
they would send those who were left behind a note—
and they did:
it was in Hebrew and all it read was: "To death."

The Jews who were left were set to dismantling the camp—
all the huts—
and in January the door of the hut they were in was suddenly opened
and a commander said, "Five out!"
The lad was among them.
There was a young doctor from Czechoslovakia among them, too,
and—in a sort of shock—
he began to sing and dance.
The driver of the truck they were in
asked the commander who was going along
where to put the Jews off
and was told, "A bit further."
There they were told to lie down
and did. As the lad was lying there
he heard the noise of bullets whizzing past—
and he, too, was shot.
The bullet came into the nape of his neck
and out through his mouth.

He was still lying there
and the officer who was shooting would pass those he had shot
and, if he saw or heard a sign of life,
would fire a second shot.
In a few minutes after the lad was shot,
he came to

[100]

and, when the officer went past, the lad held his breath
so that the officer would think he was dead.
He just kept lying there
and then there was another group of five,
and then a third.
All shot.

There was only one soldier guarding the dead
and the lad ran away when he was not looking
and hid in the stable of a non-Jew.
He stayed in the stable two days
and, when the Russians came,
was looking at them through a hole in the wall.
Somebody opened the door, came in and said to him:
"You can go out now. The Russians have come."
And he went out.
A commander of the Russians came and with him a doctor
but the doctor said there was no chance for the lad to live:
he would only live twelve or twenty-four hours at most.
The doctor thought the bullet had broken his spine.
But the bullet had just missed it,
and after thirty-six hours he was still alive.

Some Jews were still alive in the camp
just before the Russians came.
They stayed in an attic
and would not come down when the Germans ordered them to:
they saw what had happened to the others.
So the Germans brought gasoline and set the building on fire.
As far as the lad knew, only three Jews survived
of the thousands brought almost daily to the camp at Chelmno;
and he one of the three.

4

When the Germans took over the Duchy of Luxembourg
one of those deported
was sent to Theresienstadt and then to Auschwitz.
The journey to Auschwitz took two or three days.
When he went on the train in Theresienstadt
he hurried to sit near a window.

[*101*]

There were two Jews from Czechoslovakia facing him and a German
      Jew
and next to him two other Jews—three to a bench.
Before the train left they were told that it was forbidden to open
      a window
or throw anything out of it.*

It was a very warm day.
About twenty minutes after the train started,
the S.S. man on the car jumped in—
there was one in each car.
The man from Luxembourg was facing in the direction the train
      was going
and the S.S. man stood behind him
and asked, "Who opened the window?"
No one answered.
Then he asked the man who sat beside the man from Luxembourg,
"Who opened the window?"
Again there was no answer.
One of the Czech Jews had opened a parcel he had taken with him—
food for the trip—
and the S.S. man drew his pistol
and shot the Czech Jew sitting opposite the man from Luxembourg
and then the man who was sitting next to the man he had shot:
the first man was shot in the head
and the second in the neck.

The first man died at once—
his eyes still staring in fright or surprise—
and the second man lived for twelve or fifteen hours.
The others had to tie the first man to the seat
so that his body would not fall forward;

---

*At the outbreak of the Second World War there were about twenty-five hundred
Jews in the Duchy of Luxembourg besides eight hundred to two thousand refugees.
It was one of the few countries that permitted Jews to come in and these Jews
would be given visas so that they could stay and look for a new homeland. This
saved the lives of many. When the Germans took over the Duchy of Luxembourg
in October, 1941, almost seven hundred Jews were deported and of these only
thirty-six survived.

and the second man was whimpering and bleeding.
Water and first-aid bandages were in the car
but the others were not allowed to help him
and he bled to death.
Then they had to tie this man, too, to the seat
and were not allowed to open a window
as the bodies began to rot.
It became very hot during the long trip.
The S.S. man kept the lavatory for himself
and they could not use it.

They had to get off the train in a hurry—
the S.S. beating them and shouting—
and then had to line up in fours.
One of the Jews who was an inmate of the camp
came up to the man from Luxembourg
and asked if he had any money or a watch,
because if he came from Theresienstadt
he might have;
and the man from Luxembourg gave him his watch.
The other Jew, by way of thanking him, said:
"Here you have come to S.S. men.
If you are asked your profession,
say 'locksmith,' 'electrician,' or 'mechanic.'
If you are asked your age,
make it five years less.
And if you are asked if you are healthy,
say you are:
one should never be sick in this camp."
And the Jew from Luxembourg asked, "Where are we?"
And he answered, "Auschwitz."

Soon afterwards, the Jews who had been lined up went forward;
there was a table nearby
and an S.S. man seated there.
He asked each his profession and age.
Before the man from Luxembourg stood a friend of his—
his friend had been a ski champion in their home country,
        Czechoslovakia—
and when asked his profession answered, "Lawyer,"
and was sent at once to the right.
Then the man from Luxembourg was asked his profession,

and he said, "Mechanic."
"Age?"
"Thirty-eight," although he was forty-three at the time.
"Health?"
"Perfect."
The S.S. man looked him over:
his clothes dirty,
smeared with the blood of the dead men who had been in the car
    with him;
and he was hungry and thirsty.
He certainly did not look in good condition.
Then he was asked, "How long have you been at your trade?"
"Twenty-four years."
He was sent to the left—and lived.

When they were counted,
those who were sent to the left
were about two hundred
out of a transport that had numbered twelve hundred.
The rest were taken to be gassed.
As for those who came in the train that arrived right afterwards—
all were taken to be gassed at once.

Later, the two hundred that lived had to undress
and were taken to the showers;
they were clean-shaven—
all over their bodies, their heads as well—
all this with shouts and beatings.
They were then taken to a hut which had been a stable,
crowded into it,
and here spent the first few nights.
They slept without any bedding on the concrete floor
and were given the clothing given to the other prisoners—
thin striped pajamas—not flannel.
Early in the morning,
when it was still dark,
they were driven out into the open.
The roll-call went like this: "Attention.
Cap on. Cap off. Cap on. Cap off.
Quickly!"
They spent half an hour doing frog-jumps,
even in the rain and mud.

And now and then a man would be taken out of line and sent to
    the gas chambers.
If, for example, he had diarrhea—as many had—
and had to leave the drilling,
this would be recorded
and he would end up in the crematorium.

The man from Luxembourg had been registered as a mechanic
and one day a request came from the camp at Gleiwitz
for three "fine mechanics;"
he had, in fact, been a merchant—
but merchants were killed at once.
When the three arrived at Gleiwitz
the commander of the camp spoke to them
and said he wanted only qualified men
and each of them would have to prove his skill:
the other two were in fact watchmakers
and the man from Luxembourg said he was only new at the job of
    being a mechanic
but had been a nurse for the sick;
he had, in fact, studied medicine for a few semesters
and understood nursing.
He was taken to a transportation group
and his work from early morning until late at night
was to carry iron beams to the railroad cars.
At this camp, they were dismantling and assembling cannon
and manufacturing spare parts;
he carried smaller parts and the large ones, too,
from the plant to the cars.

Later Jews were taken from Gleiwitz—
sixty or seventy men on trucks—
to another camp that had been bombarded.
The trip took about two hours.
When they arrived they were told to dismantle the machines in a
    hall
and slept on the bare concrete floor.
During the day they were busy dismantling the machines
and the parts still fit for use were to be taken by freight cars to
    Gleiwitz.

They were hungry.
During the evening they were peeling potatoes for the following day
and the man from Luxembourg and the man next to him
made up their minds to hide some for themselves;
but, coming out, they were searched.
The man who had been next to the man from Luxembourg had six
    or seven potatoes in his pocket;
but the man from Luxembourg was not that clever and had only one.
Their numbers were taken down—the numbers tattooed on their
    arms—
and at the roll-call next evening
their numbers were called out by the commander in charge
and they were sentenced to death for sabotage—
the sentence to be carried out at once.

The man who had been next to the man from Luxembourg was
    hanged;
but not the usual way:
not by gallows nor by standing on a box that was pulled away from
    under him.
The rope was put around his neck and he was dragged up.
Then it was the turn of the man from Luxembourg.
The rope was around his neck when the commander said:
"Is this the man who stole only one potato?
If so," said the commander, "I will have him hanging by his hands
    for two hours."
His arms were then tied across his back
and he was pulled up.
But it seems that nature is at times kinder than human beings,
    he was to say afterwards,
for he became unconscious and stayed that way for two hours—
    or maybe days.
When he came to, he was once more on the concrete floor of the big
    hall where they dismantled the machinery
with a doctor trying to revive him and straighten out his elbows.
The next day he had to go to work again
or he would have been hanged.

On the evening before Christmas, in 1944, at Gleiwitz
they were given twice as much bread as usual
and twice as much margarine,
and something they had never been given before—jam.

On the day after Christmas, two S.S. men,
who were not usually in the camp,
came and all had to report for roll-call.
They picked out sixty or seventy men—
the man from Luxembourg among them—
and these had to go to a hut, undress,
and stand there naked.
By this time all were thin;
and half the weakest and those whose ribs were showing
were taken from the hut
and the numbers of the rest taken down.
They knew what to look for,
even if the commander—
not without showing his feeling for them—
did not tell them:
in a few days they, too, would be taken to the chimneys.

But there were no more transports from Gleiwitz to Auschwitz,
no more freight trucks to collect them.
All who had been taken out of line remained in Gleiwitz.
And, suddenly, they began hearing cannon
and there were rumors that the Russians were coming.
On a day in January,
they were ordered to get up much earlier than on other days
and were to march away;
given bread and margarine
but ordered not to touch the food until noon
because this was to be the only food they would have for the journey.
They could help each other along
but no one was to remain behind
in the belief that the Russians would find him alive.

Each had a loaf of bread
and a whole package of margarine;
wearing their clogs with wooden soles
and in their striped pajamas
and each had his blanket;
but it was January—cold and snow on the ground.
S.S. men with loaded rifles went along.
The snow stuck to the wooden soles
and the clogs became heavier and heavier
and after a while walking became so difficult

many threw away the loaves of bread
as an added burden.
They heard shooting all the time
but were ordered not to turn their heads
and knew that all who lagged behind were shot.

The man from Luxembourg began to feel sick
and his legs hurt so he could hardly walk,
but he was helped along by a companion;
perhaps because he had given him a little more soup than usual
when the doctor who had taken care of him was gone,
perhaps killed,
and for three or four days the man from Luxembourg
had acted as doctor in the camp.
Now his companion helped him along
and they trudged on that night and all of the next day
until they came to one of the camps at Auschwitz.

There were S.S. men near the gate
and a big sign,
"Work makes a man free."
The S.S. men welcomed them with beatings
because they did not come into camp singing.
A number of skulls were cracked;
the man who had been helping the man from Luxembourg
lifting his arm to cover his own head
had his arm broken.
When they came into the camp, they could smell a bean soup being
    cooked;
it smelled good, very good, but they were too tired to touch it.
They had only one wish:
to lie down and be left in peace.

An S.S. man came into the hut where they were lying
and they were told they could remain lying down the next day.
But next morning, very early, there was another roll-call
and they were told to be ready within half an hour to march again.
The man from Luxembourg could hardly lift his feet;
he would rather die there, he thought, than on the road;
and two of his acquaintances among the prisoners
also made up their minds to stay behind rather than march.

They went into another hut and decided to sleep.
All the S.S. men were on their way with those marching
and the three thought all the huts empty.
Suddenly they were awakened:
someone was shouting, "The S.S. men are back!"
In the excitement—and fear—the man from Luxembourg no longer
    felt any pain.
He and his acquaintances crossed to the public lavatories
and looked through the cracks in the walls to see what was going on:
S.S. men were shooting from the watchtowers
and had set fire to the huts where prisoners were hiding;
stood facing the doors with machine-guns
and if anyone ran out of the burning huts
he was shot,
and those who stayed inside were burned alive.
The three watching decided the S.S. men would be coming to the
    lavatories, too,
to set them on fire;
and they jumped through the seats into the pit below
and began to sink slowly into the excrement.

They could not know how deep it was
but when it reached their chests
they felt the solid ground beneath their feet.
They might have been in that pit three or five hours.
Then they heard voices
saying the S.S. men had left.

It seemed that not all the huts were on fire
and there were other prisoners left alive.
The Jewish prisoners came to help the three
and pulled them out.
It was early in the evening:
dark outside but in the winter and could not have been very late.
They cleaned themselves with snow as best they could:
there was no water.
Everywhere the smell of the burning wood of the huts
and the noise of the flames,
and the cries of those who had been burnt or shot and were still alive.
Finally the Russians came.

5

Thousands of Germans surrounded the Warsaw ghetto with
  machine-guns
and suddenly began to enter it;
those they were to hunt down
were a group of twenty or so young men and women
and between them they had only a revolver, a grenade, two guns
  and some home-made bombs—
which they had to light by matches.
But this handful who were to fight the thousands of Germans
were elated—
smiled at each other, even joked and shook hands
because they knew the Germans would pay a price for their lives.
And, after they threw their bombs and hand grenade
and there were dead and wounded among the Germans,
the commander of the Germans ordered his soldiers to collect their
  dead and wounded
and retreat.
But they came back with tanks
and the Molotov bottles of the Jews set fire to a tank.
After that the Germans came in small numbers
searching for the Jews
in cellars and attics, in dugouts and bunkers,
the Germans wearing shoes with rubber soles
and the Jews fighting them
likewise had their feet wrapped in rags
not to be heard.

There were still thousands of Jews in the ghetto—
as many as thirty or fifty thousand—
and at last to clear the ghetto of Jews
the Germans set fire to it:
at first using airplanes
and then by setting fire to building after building
until there was no longer a ghetto
but only block after block of rubble.
Not infrequently Jews stayed in the burning buildings
until, for fear of being burned alive,
they threw mattresses into the street
and jumped.
Some—with bones broken—nevertheless tried to crawl

into blocks of buildings that had not yet been set on fire
or were only partly in flames.
Often the Jews changed their hiding-places during the night
by moving into the ruins of burnt-out buildings
and hid there until found by the patrols.
Many hid in the sewers
and when their voices were heard through the sewer shafts
men of the S.S. squads or the police
climbed down the shafts to bring out the Jews.
Often they stumbled over Jews already dead;
and it was always necessary to use smoke candles
to drive the Jews out.
But a few Jews went into the sewers
to make their way out of the ghetto,
stooping in the narrow sewers
with the cold dirty water reaching their knees
and even to their lips,
and, if they could get through the Aryan part of the city,
reach the forest
where Jewish guerrillas were still fighting the Germans.*

6

Fishing boats, excursion boats, and any kind of boat
were mustered at the ports;
and the Jews were escorted to the coast by the Danes—
many of them students—
and ferried to safety in Sweden:
about six thousand Danish Jews were rescued
and only a few hundred captured by the Germans.

---

*The uprising of the Jews in the Warsaw ghetto began in the spring of 1943 and
lasted about twenty days. Of the thousands of Jews still in the ghetto when the
uprising began perhaps a few hundred escaped alive. A great number were killed by
the blowing up of their dugouts and the sewers. But, despite the burden on every
S.S. man or German police officer during these actions to drive out the Jews from
Warsaw—where they had once numbered a quarter of a million—the spirit of the
S.S. men and the police officers, it was noted by one of their superiors, was
"extraordinarily good and praiseworthy from the first day to the very last."

Printed February 1975 in Santa Barbara & Ann
Arbor for the Black Sparrow Press by Noel Young
& Edwards Brothers Inc. Typography by Graham
Mackintosh. Design by Barbara Martin. This
edition is published in paper wrappers; there are 250
hardcover copies numbered & signed by the poet; &
35 copies handbound in boards by Earle Gray each
with a holograph poem by Charles Reznikoff.

Photo: Gerard Malanga

Charles Reznikoff was born in a Jewish ghetto in Brooklyn in 1894. His parents were immigrants from Russia. He was graduated from the Brooklyn Boys' High School when not quite sixteen, spent a year at the new School of Journalism of the University of Missouri (1910-1911), and entered the law school of New York University in 1912. Admitted to the bar of the State of New York in 1916, he practiced only briefly. The United States had entered the First World War and in 1918 he was admitted to the officers' training camp at Columbia University, but before he received any training the war was over. His parents were then in business as manufacturers of hats and, for a while, he was a salesman for them, selling to jobbers and large department stores. In 1928, he went to work writing law for the firm publishing *Corpus Juris*, an encyclopedia of law for lawyers. Later, he worked in Hollywood for about three years for a friend who was then a producer for Paramount Pictures. After that, he made his living by freelance writing, research, translating, and editing. In 1962, New Directions published a selection of his verse, *By the Waters of Manhattan*. He was awarded the Jewish Book Council of America's award for English poetry in 1963 and in 1971 the Morton Dauwen Zabel Award for Poetry by the National Institute of Arts and Letters.

He was married in 1930 to Marie Syrkin, now Professor Emeritus of Humanities, Brandeis University.

In 1975 Black Sparrow Press will begin publication of Charles Reznikoff's *Complete Poems*, edited by Seamus Cooney.